To: Tracie

Thank you for all your support.
I pray this book blesses you.

5am with GOD...

Build a Closer Relationship with God

Keaires Roberson

Author Photo: Dokk Savage Photography
Book Cover Design: Studio 5 Agency

Printed in the United States of America
ISBN 978-1979224253
Keen Vision Publishing, LLC
www.keen-vision.com

For my son, Jaden. You motivate me more than you will ever know. I love you!

Contents

Introduction

"But seek ye first the kingdom of God and his righteousness, and all of these things will be added to you."

Matthew 6:33 (NKJV)

Broken. Hurt. Confused. Lost. Can you imagine wandering through life clueless about who you are and what you should be doing in life? Can you imagine constantly walking around feeling as if your very existence is a mistake? That was me for most of my life. I felt as if there was no help for me. I felt like I was in a constant downward spiral with no way out. I had no clue about my purpose. I often questioned why I even existed. I was broken, and I felt defeated. I knew I was not living the life God had planned for me, but I had no clue how to find His will and get into it.

I wish I could tell you that I went on a seven day fast, and all of a sudden I was made whole, but this was not the case. For me, I got connected to individuals who refused to allow me to stay where I was. I got connected to people who saw more in me than I saw in myself. I began to be intentional about seeking God. I found myself studying and seeking Him at 5 a.m. I know you're probably thinking, "What? 5 a.m.? There's no way I'm getting up that early!" I even thought this way at first. Once my mind adjusted, I realized that seeking God early in the day allowed me to have a more productive day.

This stretched me to be more disciplined in the time I went to bed, and also allowed me to prepare for my day better. As a bonus, the more I studied God's Word and drew closer to Him, He began to show me my identity. He also allowed me to see that others suffered from understanding who they were created to be. I can honestly say that now, I am free. I understand who I am and who God has called me to be. After every 5 a.m. encounter with Him, I learned more and more about what He has created me to do. My entire life has been shifted and transformed. My perspective about everything has changed. I believe, think, work, and even dress differently! Those encounters with God resulted in this very book.

5 a.m. with God is designed to help you grow closer to God. This book discusses vital areas we need to understand on our walk with Christ. My prayer is that you will experience the abundance of God in love, peace, wisdom, and knowledge. So many times, we look for a Word or for a new program to change our lives. While these are amazing, nothing beats spending quiet, uninterrupted, and intentional time with God in His Word and His presence.

After reading this book, I pray that you will begin to seek God intentionally. Maybe your time won't be 5a.m., but it is very important that you find uninterrupted time to spend in the presence of God.

Chapter One

How to Fight

Wake up! Wake up! Yes, I know 5 a.m. is early. I also know the enemy does not get tired. So, why not have an advantage over the enemy? Wake up and get in the presence of God. First and foremost, we do not fight physically. You will never win or get anything accomplished fist fighting the enemy. The enemy is not concerned with how many punches you can throw, or how well you can curse someone out. He knows those actions will only hinder and distract you. When we fight with fists and profanity, we make his job easier. Hang up your boxing gloves, wash your mouth with soap, and allow me to teach you how to win!

Let's start with your eating habits. Professional boxers have a very strict diet. Their diets are designed to keep them limber and energetic when they are in the ring. When it comes to warfare in the spirit, your physical diet is important as well! So, what are your eating habits like? Are you continually shoving garbage down your throat? Do you eat whatever you want to eat whenever you want to eat? That was once me. I couldn't figure out why my judgment was so cloudy. I could not produce what needed to be produced because I was constantly filling my body with garbage. When you consume garbage, you produce garbage. I'm not saying the food you eat will hinder your relationship with God. What I am saying is that your transition into a place of closeness with Him will go a lot smoother if you consider what you put into your body.

"Their destiny is destruction, their god is their stomach, and their glory is in their shame. Their mind is set on earthly things."

Philippians 3:19 (NIV)

Is your stomach your god? Does your stomach control you? Do you have to have what you want when you want it? God had to check me when it came to food. Let's just be honest, we all love food. I was so concerned with what I was going to eat. I was thinking about dinner for the next day before the next day even arrived. And not because I was super planned and organized, but because I was greedy. I am now a pescatarian. Do not stop eating meat on account of me. If you know you are abusing certain foods, it may be time to hang it up. Once my diet changed, my hearing, thinking, and the way I viewed God changed. My judgment was no longer cloudy.

If you are serious about your new journey, there are things you are going to have to give up. Liquor used to be mine. I would drink every single day of the week, and no one ever knew. I would sit at home in front my T.V. and drink Crown and Coke! I wasn't hurting anyone, so I thought. In all honesty, I was hurting me, God, and my family. Our body is God's temple, and He does not want us to destroy it. I thought I was functioning fine. I could still go to work, school, etc. I was blind to the spirit. It looked as if I was walking through smog, or a cloud of smoke. I would cry out," Where are you, God? Why are you not answering me?" All along, He was standing right there. I was just too drunk to see Him. What is holding you down? What is keeping you from your destiny? Your family cannot get free until you get free. Are you too drunk to break the barrier?

In your attempt to build a closer relationship with God, don't forget to take a look at the things you are consuming on a daily basis. There are many new health plans trending in this day and age. Be careful not to pick one because it's what everyone else is doing. Seek God on the things you need to remove from your daily diet.

Using the lines below, write about the adjustments you will need to make in your life to improve your ability to fight!

_____

_____

_____

_____

_____

_____

_____

_____

_____

_____

_____

_____

_____

_____

_____

_____

Keaires Roberson

Chapter Two

Prayer

How should we pray, you ask? First, allow me to make this disclaimer. If you are a beginner in prayer, it does not mean that you cannot pray. You have an advantage because you, my friend, can start from scratch. Starting out a prayer is as simple as having a conversation with your friend. God will meet you where you are. You can start small and build your endurance in prayer daily. Prayer is all about conversing with God. In the same way that you would call you friends to talk about your day, try telling God about your day. Communicate with Him about the details of your day just as you would talk with your friends. Continue doing that every day. After you have gotten comfortable doing that, start setting aside prayer time. No T.V. and no noise – just you and the Father. Next, begin to pray scripture. God is His word, and He wants us to pray His Word back to Him. Ex. John 15:7 (NIV) says, "If you remain in me and my words remain in you, ask whatever you wish, and it will be done for you." Take that scripture go to

God in prayer and say, "Lord you said: If I remain in you, you will remain in me and that I can ask for whatever I wish and it will be done for me. Show me how I can remain in you." Sounds fancy, doesn't it? You did not do anything hard. You are bringing God's Word back to Him. God will move when you pray His word. Why? Because it is His Word, and His Word shall not return unto Him void. There is a scripture for everything you are dealing with and everything you have gone through. Google is your friend. Google the scripture, go to the Bible, then apply it to the situation at hand.

Now that we have that out of the way, this is when you sit still. After you've prayed, listen! This is the most important part of prayer, however, many people forget this part. After you've spoken to God, be quiet and listen for what He has to say to you. Remember, prayer is a conversation, a dialogue. Wait for God to talk back to you. It may be audible, through a book, through a song, or through other people, but He does talk back. God does not want your quickies. Therefore, be intentional about making time for Him. If you do not hear God during your prayer time, listen throughout the day for Him. God is always talking. The question is, are you listening?

Using the lines below, write some prayers to God. Don't forget to use scriptures!

_____

_____

_____

_____

_____

_____

_____

_____

_____

_____

_____

_____

_____

_____

_____

_____

Keaires Roberson

Chapter Three

Fasting

I f you are not a Bible reader, now is a good time to start. Throughout the entire Bible, we see many people fasting and going before the Lord. Esther fasted because she had an assignment, and she knew what had to be fulfilled. The Ninevites were able to turn their lives around through prayer and fasting. Daniel fasted for 21 days. Some things will only come through fasting and prayer. Fasting is giving up something good for something better. There are many types of fasts. In the Biblical days, they mainly fasted from food and people. Isolation during fasting can be very helpful. Fasting is essential for your relationship with God. Put down the phone, get off social media, and turn off the T.V. A lot of times we miss God because of distractions. Take time away from those things to spend time with God. Decide in your heart how long to fast, when to fast, listen for God to tell you when to fast, or even if your church is doing a corporate fast. When you start a fast, try to follow through. Ecclesiastes 5:5 (NIV) states, "It is better not to make a vow than to make one and not fulfill it." In most cases, the most effective fast is food. When you do not intake food, not only can you see clearer, but you hear clearer. God is a spirit, so He does not have to eat food to survive. Our bodies, believe it or not, can go a substantial amount of time without food. I've noticed that when I fast from food, I hear God more frequently. He gives me fresh revelation in my time of fasting that had I not been fasting, I would have probably missed. If you are new to fasting, give up what you love. If sweet tea is your thing, go without it for a few days, you will be fine. Maybe it's not sweet tea, but you must have a steak and loaded baked potato often. Skip that meal a few times. I promise you will not die. There are also other fasts you can do such as the Daniel fast. You can find it in the book of Daniel in the Bible, which you are going to start reading today, right? Having a purpose for fasting is good. Other than fasting from people and things, you should be fasting to be alone and to draw closer to God. When we fast, we deny our flesh of the things it desires. It is important that we replace our fleshly desires with prayer, reading God's Word, and spending time in God's presence. Fasting is a time of intimacy with just you and God. He will reveal things to you. With distractions and food out of the way, it will not be hard for you to hear God clearly about things concerning your life.

Do you need to go on a fast? Probably so! Use the lines below to create a fasting schedule!

_____

_____

_____

_____

_____

_____

_____

_____

_____

_____

_____

_____

_____

_____

_____

_____

_____

_____

Keaires Roberson

Chapter Four

Relationship

Whenever you are in a healthy relationship with someone you love, you call and check on them daily, right? Not only do you tell them you love them, but you also show them. That is how God wants our relationship to be with Him. He loves us, and He gave His only Son to save us. I have yet to meet anyone willing to give up their child for others. I don't know about you, but I don't think I would be able to sacrifice my own son. The love God has for us is unexplainable. So, how do we love God? By keeping His commands, as well as loving others and doing what's right. God meets people where they are. He understands that you may not have as much knowledge and intellect concerning the Bible. That does not make Him love you less, and that does not make the person who has a degree in theology better than you. God loves you unconditionally.

Another way to build your relationship with God is through worship. When we worship God, we think about his splendor and His goodness. We reverence Him and tell Him how amazing He is to us. God, you are amazing! God, you are my everything! God, I love you! God, I need you! God is a forgiving God. God wants to hear us speak well of Him from a genuine place in our hearts.

Religion is the exact opposite of having a relationship with God. Religion condemns and makes us feel as if we're going straight to hell no matter what you do. Religion judges beyond measure. My Pastor once said, "Religion condemns people for drinking out in a public place, while they drink a whole bottle of liquor behind closed doors." Matthew 7:5 (NIV) says, "You hypocrite, first take the plank out of your own eye, and then you will see clearly to remove the speck from your brother's eye." In this scripture, God is saying stop condemning people for the same thing you are doing. Religion makes you feel as if you have to be perfect. Some religions even state that you must dress a certain type of way, and if you do not, you are considered unholy. I have been in church my whole life. I was religious because that's all I had seen. In 2016, I was delivered from that religious demon, Now I can say I love people, show it, and actually mean it.

So, before you get all tied up in the rules of religion, focus on having a relationship with the Father. Following the rules of religion won't change your heart, only an encounter with God can do this. You can have daily encounters with the Father by building a relationship with Him.

Using the lines below, write how you plan to improve your relationship with God.

_____

_____

_____

_____

_____

_____

_____

_____

_____

_____

_____

_____

_____

_____

_____

_____

_____

_____

Keaires Roberson

Chapter Five

Discouragement

If you have been reading this book and taking the necessary steps I've mentioned in previous chapters, then right about now you may be feeling a little discouraged. Maybe you feel like you keep messing up. Maybe you even feel like you can't seem to get this thing right. Maybe you've been setting your alarm clock and still can't seem to get up early enough to spend time with God. If that's the case, rest assured that everything you are experiencing is normal. Whenever we decide to make a difference in our lives for the best, the enemy goes into overtime. Don't ever mistake the enemy for being stupid. He is cunning and clever. He sees you studying, finding out who you are, and tapping into your gifts. So, guess what? That is his cue to ATTEMPT to steal, kill, and destroy. Whatever you do, don't allow his attempts to discourage you and get you off track make you quit! Keep pressing and trying harder. Do not allow life and circumstances to discourage you. Keep going! You've got this! As Christians, we sometimes make the mistake of believing that when we

21

encounter hardships or obstacles, that is a sign to turn around and go back. This is not true. The closer we get to the things God desires for us, the more the enemy will throw our way. But fret not, dear one. 2 Corinthians 12:9 (NIV) encourages us in this, "But he said to me, "My grace is sufficient for you for my power is made perfect in weakness." God is at His strongest during our times of weakness. Stop allowing your emotions to control you. Anytime I feel defeated, sad, upset, etc. I say, "Emotions, I command you to come under subjection to the Holy Spirit that lives on the inside of me." Try it. It works! Who's bigger? Your emotions or God? In your moments of despair, lean on God. Don't try to keep going in your own strength. Tap into the strength of God that lives on the inside of you!

Have you been feeling discouraged lately? Using the lines below, write some action steps you will take to change your attitude.

_____

_____

_____

_____

_____

_____

_____

_____

_____

_____

_____

_____

_____

_____

_____

_____

_____

Keaires Roberson

Chapter Six

Fellowship

Anybody who knows me can tell you that I was once standoffish, cold, and I sometimes came off as mean. Once I started going to the church I attend now, God changed that. My church is full of huggers; that's just what we do. I used to hate it when people touched me, nevertheless hug me. Eventually, I got used to the hugs and love and I started giving them out. First things first, if you do not have a church home, start seeking for one now. Fellowship is super important. I do not care how strong you are, or how much you think you can do it on your own, we all need somebody. In your search for a church home, it is imperative that the Pastor hears from God! Be sure they are hearing what the Lord is saying now. You do not want to end up in a place of stagnation.

How will you know if it is the right church for you? Whelp, I'm glad you asked!

1. Pray about it.
2. Get still and listen for God.
3. Fast on it.

25

4. Keep your eyes and ears open for confirmation.

I've made some real-life connections since I have been connected to my current place of worship. The Woman to Woman Single Moms group is another group I joined. Being a part of this group has been extraordinary to me. It's a group full of other single mother's, like myself, that God allowed me to be a part of. The mom who is over the group has made things happen on my behalf. I am most grateful for these women. Had I not taken the time to talk to people and allow new people into my life, I would not be a part of such an amazing group. I also teach in the children's ministry at my local church. Typically, when I think of children's ministry, the first thing that comes to my mind is hotdogs and coloring sheets. So not the case at our church. We TEACH the kids. We do activities, pray with them, and ask questions. Our teachers are more concerned about their souls versus just passing the time. The director of the children's ministry shows her concerns for the teachers as well. We have life projects entitled streams. Streams are different ways to build additional income and to help with life overall. Streams helped me to clean out my closets, cut down on bills, create better spending habits, and it helped me to become a better person. Anytime I have a problem or just need to vent, the people in this ministry are available. Wow! A children's ministry that helps you, while you're helping the children. Imagine that! I know what you're thinking. Kids are not my thing, so why would I want to join the children's ministry? Hey, guess what? It was not mine either, but God said otherwise. There are different kinds of ministries in the church. Allow God to speak to you and tell you what it is you need to be doing. In the meantime, get connected and soak in all you can. Make new friends and go to the movies with one another; it is okay. Use your discernment and enjoy life. Do not rush yourself to certain areas in the church. God will let you know exactly where He wants you in due time. Fellowship with others and my church family has changed my life. It will change yours if you allow it to. Work the process; there is no way around it. You can only go through it.

Using the lines below, write about the different areas in your church you would like to volunteer with and why.

_____

_____

_____

_____

_____

_____

_____

_____

_____

_____

_____

_____

_____

_____

_____

_____

_____

_____

_____

5am with God

Keaires Roberson

Chapter Seven

Holy Spirit

I feel as if I'm doing this all alone. Nobody cares, no one understands." We've all been guilty of saying these words, but this statement is so far from the truth. Why? Because Jesus promised us the Holy Spirit. John 14:16 (NIV) says, "And I will ask the Father, and he will give you another advocate to help you and be with you forever- the spirit of truth." Jesus tells us in His Word that the world cannot accept the Holy Spirit because they do not know Him. But with you being a believer, you know Him, so He lives in you. If you are not sure if you are filled with the Holy Spirit, speak these words, "I confess with my mouth and heart that the Lord is my savior. I believe that He sent His only Son, Jesus, to die for my sins, and save me so that I may have eternal life. Holy Spirit, I invite you in to live, move, and dwell on the inside of me." Jesus promised he would not leave us as orphans. He knew He had to leave, that's why He left the Holy Spirit as a gift. The Holy Spirit does many things. He is a teacher, a guide, and a manual for your life. John 14:26 states, "But the Advocate, the Holy Spirit, whom the Father will send in my name, will teach you all things and will remind you of everything I have said to you." Can I testify about Holy Spirit? I sure can! Early on in 2016, my cousin told me I would be doing my hair. I rebuked her! I said, "I will never do my hair. I do not know how to do my hair, and I can't do a curl to save my life!" I was so upset with her for delivering to me what the Lord had given her. In my mind, the Lord did not tell her such foolishness. And sure enough, she heard correctly. The Holy Spirit started to tell me to watch YouTube videos on hair. At first, I was like okay, cool. Then I thought of the conversation that my cousin and I initially had. After watching countless hours of videos, the Holy Spirit spoke to me and said, "Start doing your hair."

I yelled out, "What? You do know I don't know what I'm doing, right?"

The Holy Spirit replied, "I am going to help you."

I did better than any professional that has ever done my hair. The Holy Spirit will help you with anything. And if that was not mind-blowing enough for you, I can minister to married couples. I have never been married, but for some reason, married couples always seek me for advice. I remember when I would I sit and speak with couples and the Holy Spirit would just pour the words right out of my mouth.

The Holy Spirit is your strength. Do not try to do anything without it, and I mean anything. Try me on this; the Holy Spirit is available to help you, not harm you.

Using the lines below, write about your experience with the Holy Spirit. Also, write a few ways you can tap into the Holy Spirit daily.

_____

_____

_____

_____

_____

_____

_____

_____

_____

_____

_____

_____

_____

_____

_____

_____

_____

_____

Keaires Roberson

Chapter Eight

Idols

When you hear the word idol, what first comes to your mind? A statue of some sort, right? Though an idol can be a statue, there are other kinds of idols as well. An idol is anything or anyone that you give more time to than you give God. Yes, that's exactly what I'm saying. Your child, job, food, and even your house can become idols. If you find yourself obsessing over something constantly, check it. Some do not intentionally idolize things, but sometimes, it just happens that way. If God is important to you, make time. The funny thing is we have time for everything, but God. Some may say that is not true. We make sure we go to work, we clean up, and find time to spend with the family. Some of us even serve in a ministry in our local churches. That doesn't leave a whole lot of time for Jesus, does it? America's most prominent idol is food. I do not care what time of the day it is or where you are, food is always on the human mind. Who's drive-thru am I going to go to? What am I going to eat once church lets out? Philippians 3:19 (NIV) says, "Their destiny is destruction, their god is their stomach, and their glory is in their shame. Their mind is set on earthly things." Our stomach should not tell us what to do, and we definitely should not have our minds set on earthly things. It is time to get out of self and get into God. Take a moment and reevaluate your life. Are you idolizing anything? If you are, or if you feel as if you are, cut time back with that certain thing or certain person. God is a jealous God. The Creator should not have to fight for time to spend with His creation. Give God more of you!

Do you have any idols in your life? Using the lines below, write about how you will seek God to remove these idols.

_____

_____

_____

_____

_____

_____

_____

_____

_____

_____

_____

_____

_____

_____

_____

_____

_____

_____

_____

_____

Chapter Nine

Singleness

This chapter is for my single men and women! If you are married, keep reading, this is not your cue to stop. What's so great about being single? In your singleness, you must only answer to God. I'm not saying you can't receive advice from others, but once God speaks a thing, that's it! I have been single for almost four years. It has been a rough, but incredible journey. When it's time to sow into someone's life, I get to do it freely. Of course, with God's okay. Most of the time, God will tell you when and when not to sow. If I were married, I would have to check with my husband first. Guess what? 1 Corinthians 7:8, 32, 34 (NIV) says, "Now to the unmarried and the widows I say: It is good for them to stay unmarried as I do. I would like you to be free from concern. An unmarried man is concerned about the Lord's affairs-how can he please the Lord. An unmarried woman or virgin is concerned about the Lord's affairs: Her aim is to be devoted to the Lord in both body and spirit. But a married woman is concerned about the affairs of this world and how she can please her husband." Whether male or female, when we are single, we can give God our undivided attention.

Being single has its perks as well as lonely days. Sometimes, I find myself longing for a significant other, and other days, I couldn't care less. I am now at a point in my life, where it does not make a difference whether I'm single or not. If you are obsessing over being married in your singleness, sit down, you aren't ready. If you are already giving more time to this ideal mate in your mind, why would God send the real thing to you? So that you can continue to avoid Him like you've been doing? Apply that same effort and time into the Lord. The peace and joy I have gained in my singleness came through the Lord. You must learn to be content with just you and God before He sends the one.

Another perk of being single is that I can do what God tells me without having to ask anyone else for permission. I just do it. God told me to drop everything, not to pick up shifts at my job for three days, turn off my television, phone, social media, etc. I did it with no hesitation. When I wrote this book, I went on a three-day fast from everything. God needed me secluded so He could share some very vital things with me. If I were married, this task probably would have been impossible. In your single stage, embrace being single and spend time with God to get to know Him better. Get to know you better.

Are you currently single? Using the lines below, write how you can take advantage of your season of singleness.

_____

_____

_____

_____

_____

_____

_____

_____

_____

_____

_____

_____

_____

_____

_____

_____

_____

Keaires Roberson

Chapter Ten

Who Are You?

I always ask my students, "Who are you?" Their response is their name. Your name does not define who you are. If you were thinking your name when you read the title of this chapter, push that thought to the back of your mind. A name without character and perseverance means absolutely nothing. For a long time, I went through life by name. In my eyes, I was fat, unlovable, ugly, and did not amount to anything. Even the dogs were higher than me, so I thought. I did not find out who I was until I met Jesus. Knowing who you are is going to make this process a whole lot easier.

How do you find yourself?

1. Stop competing and comparing
2. Be yourself
3. Speak over your life what God says about you
4. Release yourself from toxic people who mean you know good.

If you apply these four steps to your life, you will begin to love you. My Pastor once said, "The only person you need

to compete with is you! Be better than you were yesterday."
He is exactly right. If God wanted you to be Beyoncé, He
would have created two Beyoncé's. Be unique. Be different.
There is something on the inside of you (yes, you!) that God
wants to use. If you are trying to do the very same thing the
person next to you is doing, you have lost your originality.
God did not create us to be like the little yellow Minions,
walking around looking the same. When you imitate others,
you are setting yourself up for failure. How? Because they
are anointed for that. God has graced them to do the things
they are operating in, not you! What works for them may not
work for you. Find your lane and walk in it. Some of you
may be asking, "What does God say about me?"
Deuteronomy 28:13 says the Lord will make you the head
and not the tail. Ephesians 2:10 tells us we are God's
handiwork. Zechariah 2:8 tells us that we are the apple of
God's eye. God loves us in ways we cannot imagine, but
unless you read His Word, you will never know. Do not call
it strange if you are now dressing, eating, and responding
differently than you normally would. I vowed never to wear
another heel. God has changed my whole wardrobe. I am
now wearing heels, dresses, and skirts.

When trying to find out who you are, you must be willing
to allow God to transform every area of your life. If you
allow Him, I promise He will. Spend some time learning
who God has created you to be. Once you find your true
identity, hold on tight to it! Don't let it go or convince
yourself to be like anyone else! God made you on purpose,
for a purpose.

Do you know who you are? Using the lines below, write about who you were before you encountered God, and who you are now.

_____

_____

_____

_____

_____

_____

_____

_____

_____

_____

_____

_____

_____

_____

_____

_____

_____

_____

_____

_____

Keaires Roberson

Chapter Eleven

Accountability Partner

An accountability partner is a person who coaches another person to keep a commitment. I do not care who you are, we all need an accountability partner. There is a need for at least one person we can trust and share things with. Being able to be open and share things as the Lord gives them unto you can be extremely helpful and encouraging in your walk with God. I am grateful to have an accountability partner who is able to push me through when I feel stuck. It keeps me going. Romans 2:13 tells us it's not those who hear the word who are righteous, but those who obey it. An accountability partner helps keep you in line and your spirit in check. If you do not have an accountability partner, begin to seek one out now. Seek God's guidance about who would make a good accountability partner. Here are a few things you should look for in an accountability partner:

1. Do they know more than you concerning the Bible?
2. Are they in tune with what God is saying now?
3. How do they treat God's people?
4. Are they connected to a church?

You cannot just choose anyone to hold you accountable during your walk with God. Everyone does not have your best interest at heart. Sometimes, you will want to operate off the world's system. You will need someone to pull you back in and tell you, "No, I'm not going to let you destroy yourself." I know in this generation, we yell no new friends, but we need new friends. Some of our old ones do not have enough power to help get us to our destiny. Do not feel bad for disconnecting the old and connecting with the new. It is vital for your life. If you have an accountability partner who does not meet the criteria above, they are negative and it is time for a new accountability partner. Outgrowing that person is possible. Hebrews 10:24-25 (NIV) says, "And let us consider how we may spur one another on toward love and good deeds, not giving up meeting together, as some are in the habit of doing, but encouraging one another-and all the more as you see the day approaching." This is what God wants for us. If you are closed up, now is the time to open up. I am not saying spill the beans to everyone you meet, but sit down with the Father and talk about your new or current accountability partner.

What type of people are in your circle? Using the lines below, write about those you spend time with and what they add to your life.

_____

_____

_____

_____

_____

_____

_____

_____

_____

_____

_____

_____

_____

_____

_____

_____

_____

_____

Keaires Roberson

Chapter Twelve

Misunderstood

By now, some of your family and friends probably think you are crazy. They think you have gone coo-coo for cocoa puffs, and that is okay. It is not a bad thing; it's a sign that you are on the right track with God. Sometimes, God will give you something that other people will not understand. They may even try to discredit God or tell you it isn't God. Just because others do not agree doesn't mean it's not God. As you grow higher in God, there will be people who will not understand you and they will think you are crazy. You may even feel crazy some days, but that's when you will know you have tapped into God. Man will try to make sense of what God has given you. Speaking from experience, 75% of the time, what God does in my life does not make sense to me. Isaiah 55:8 (NIV) says, "For my thoughts are not your thoughts, neither are your ways my ways. Declares the Lord." When I started getting revelation from God, and He began speaking to me and using me, some of the people around me made me feel small and as if I was not hearing God. At one point, I became so intimidated that

I would not even open my mouth. Now, you cannot shut me up! When God tells me to speak, I do so without hesitation! Ephesians 1:9 (NIV) says, "He made known to us the mystery of his will according to his good pleasure, which he purposed in Christ." Ephesians 3:4-5 (NIV) says, "In reading this, then you will be able to understand my insight into the mystery of Christ. Which was not made known to people in other generations as it has now been revealed by the Spirit to God's holy apostles and prophets." Those verses tell us everything we need to know. You do not need to slow down; the people around you need to catch up. They do not comprehend or receive what God is doing in you for many reasons:

1. They are not you!
2. God did not ask them. People feel as if God has to check with them first concerning you!
3. They are too focused on your relationship with Christ versus their own. If they were tapped in, seeking and finding as they should be, they would not have enough time to be so focused on you.

What had God assigned you to do? Using the lines below, write about your God-given assignment and what you will do to stay focused on what He has called you to do.

_____

_____

_____

_____

_____

_____

_____

_____

_____

_____

_____

_____

_____

_____

_____

_____

_____

_____

_____

Keaires Roberson

Chapter Thirteen

Power

Y ou should be feeling pretty powerful! There is no way you can grow closer to God and not obtain power. Luke 10:19 (NIV) says, "I have given you authority to trample on snakes and scorpions and to overcome all the power of the enemy nothing will harm you." Why do we need power over the enemy? I'm glad you asked! Demons are real; demonic spirits are real. In your spare time, read Matthew, Mark, and Luke. Those books talk about how Jesus cast out demons, healed, and made people whole. Jesus' disciples also did the same things. Because you are a disciple of the Lord, the Bible says that you will do even GREATER works! Yes, you!

I've seen demonic spirits on people. I have dealt with a tormenting spirit in my house. I have experienced encounters with demonic spirits. So yes, they are very real. One day, I approached an unruly child, spoke, and said, "You rebellious spirit! I command you to come out of him in Jesus name!" It recognized the God in me, and also told me it was not going to come out. In situations like these, you must keep speaking and praying; it's not going to leave willingly. When a tormenting spirit was in my house, I felt as if someone was standing over me. I would constantly hear noises that I would not normally hear. I began praying over my house and speaking the Word of God over my house. The spirit could not stay any longer. 2 Timothy 1:7 (NIV) says, "For the Spirit of God gave us does not make us timid, but gives us power, love and self-discipline." Was I afraid when I first started experiencing this stuff? Of course! But I was reminded by God that this is what I was supposed to be doing. This is not strange. If you are supposed to be doing greater works than Jesus did, why wouldn't you be casting out demons? You have dominion over them! You have the power to shift atmospheres, and change situations. Even at your weakest, you are powerful! Why? Because God dwells in you and you in Him. He is all knowing and almighty! No, you are not God, but you are God's image. The enemy job is to kill, steal, and destroy. Your job is to save souls. Embrace your power!

Are there some areas in your life where you need to apply the power given to you? Using the lines below, write how you will use the power you have to change the trajectory of your life!

_____

_____

_____

_____

_____

_____

_____

_____

_____

_____

_____

_____

_____

_____

_____

_____

_____

_____

Keaires Roberson

Chapter Fourteen

Trust God

Trusting God is easier said than done. With all that you have read and taken in, trusting God at this point should not be a struggle for you. I can honestly say I just started trusting God in 2016. Allow me to take you back for a moment. Between the ages of nine and eleven, I was molested; not just once, but multiple times and on separate occasions. One of those men was my biological father, and the other one was a friend of the family at the time. As a child, it traumatized me. I was angry with the world, myself, the men who hurt me, my mother, and God. I fell into a deep depression. I began to think I was ugly, fat, and worthless. I wrote out a suicide letter and planned to end my life. The only thing that kept me alive was the thought, "I can't leave my brothers and sisters behind. Someone has to protect them." Being raped held a stronghold over my life. The older I got, the louder the voices became. Sometimes, when it was time to bathe, I would get sick at the sight of my body. Not because anything was wrong, but I was disgusted with the reoccurring thoughts that haunted my mind day and night. I entered a controlling relationship at the age of 17. He was abusive verbally, mentally, but never physically. I soon found out that verbal abuse was a lot worse. My identity was stolen when I was nine, so I was an easy target. I stayed with this man for three years. Some days were good, and other days I felt like the scum of the earth. I allowed it because I loved him. And if that was not enough, I left that relationship and entered into another relationship with a drug dealer. I saw and did some things for a long time. One day, I packed up, moved away, and found a loving church home. I was Humpty Dumpty, and they helped put me back together again. Even in this instance, I still was not free. I often found myself worried sick about my son's wellbeing. I would call and check on my son every few hours. I would not let him go outside without me. I would tell the daycare teachers to make sure they took him to the women's restroom. While working my shift, my mind would race with all the things that could go wrong. I watched his every move. I smothered him. He was only allowed to go with a select few. I was a train wreck with no horn, and I suffered silently. The people around me had no idea, and apparently neither did I.

God uprooted me from the church I was at and placed me where I am now. That's when my deliverance came. God opened my eyes to a whole new light. I found myself taking advice from friends and family concerning my child. God placed me around people who loved me back to health. The love I receive at my place of worship is unreal. My Pastor did not speak to my flesh, he spoke to my spirit. He spoke to the Keaires I was created to be! My Pastor always says,

"Nothing happens to you; it happens for you." God had to tell me, "I knew your son before I gave him to you. I love him more than you do. I knew him before I even placed him in your womb. Let me be God; I do not need your help. You are going to have to trust me with all things, including your son. And even if something does happen, I am still God. I see all and know all."

From that point on, I experienced real freedom. I trust God with my life, my son, bills, family, etc. When did I realize I had begun to trust God? When I started allowing my son to go outside by himself. He rides the school bus from school. He walks to school with his friends in the morning. When he goes to school, I do not call. I work my shift in peace now. I finally trust God. Trusting God will take you places money can't. Maybe my story is similar to yours. If you do not remember anything I have said to you, remember this: God loves you so much that He sent his only son to die for you! He deserves your trust.

Do you have trust issues? Using the lines below, write about the areas in which you find difficulty trusting God. How do you plan to relinquish your control to God?

Acknowledgements

First and foremost, I give thanks to the head of my life, my Lord and Savior Jesus Christ. Without God, this book would not be possible. I would like to acknowledge my mother, friends, and family. Thank you all for pushing me to be the best version of myself. I would also like to acknowledge my pastor, Adrian Davis and my All Nations Worship Assembly-HSV church family. Thank each of you for pushing me out of my comfort zone!

About the Author

Keaires Roberson is an outgoing, hands-on, lover of people. She is a lover of Christ and a firm believer of His Word. Keaires is a woman of great integrity and a God chaser. She loves to sing, cook, and write poetry in her spare time. She has successfully completed the Music Majors Vocal Training, with recording artist, Jeremy Kelsey. Keaires obtained a certificate from Who's Who Among Students in American Universities & Colleges from John. C. Calhoun Community College due to her accomplishments as a student.

Keaires possesses the ability to meet people where they are in life. She can be a bit of a goof ball, playful, serious, kind, authoritative, loyal, and down to earth. She has a total of seven brothers and sisters. Keaires is a single mother of one amazing little boy. She is overall a pretty amazing person.

In the future, Keaires plans to start organizations geared towards helping people tap into who God has created them to be, and walk boldly in their purpose.

Stay Connected

FACEBOOK Keaires Roberson
INSTAGRAM @keaires02
WEBSITE www.keairesroberson.com